"いそがしい わんこの いちにち" 書評
Praise for "*Doggy's Busy Day*"

「この本を読んでると、犬のエラと一緒に子供達も冒険に出かけてるみたいなの。そんな感じのかわいらしい本よ。お話の流れやところどころに入る質問と形式おかげで、まるで自分も本の中にいるみたいに感じるのね。子供達もエラと一緒に冒険に出て、ストーリーの一部になってるみたいな。読者の子供達が犬を飼ってる、飼ってないに関わらず楽しめるの。本当に素敵な本よ。」クリスティーナ・チェリス、カオラス（Christiana Caeliss, Caolas）

"A sweet book for children that takes them on an adventure with Ella the dog. Because of the format and the questions asked, it as interactive as one can have in a book. Children can go on an adventure with Ella as they can see themselves right in the story. Whether the young reader has a dog or not, this is a delightful book that will bring joy to many young hearts." ~ Christiana Caeliss, Caolas

「ジェイン・フラーガン の "いそがしい わんこの いちにち" は、愛らしいハスキー犬の写真も入っていて、幼い子供達を惹き付ける本よ。文章がシンプルだからって内容もシンプルだと思っちゃダメよ。ページ毎に読者への問いかけが入ってるから、普段の自分たちを思い返して、ああだよね、こうだよね、なんて、本の中味を超えて、読んであげてる大人と子供達がいろいろ話したりできるの。それに、この本のストーリーは犬の普通の一日に沿って構成されているのね。読者からすれば、話に付いて行きやすい構成なの。幼い子供達が物事を学ぶのにはとても大事なことよ。楽しんでね！」ドナ・キムブランド（Donna Kim-Brand）

"Doggy's Busy Day" by Jayne Flaagan is an appealing book for young children, supported by photos of her adorable husky dog. Don't let the simple format fool you into thinking this is a passive read. The questions embedded in each page invite engagement and consideration by the youngsters and their adult reading companions relevant to their own life, possibly extending into more complex conversations over time. What's more, the book is structured to take the doggie through a normal day, which can provide a parallel support structure for the reader. These elements are crucial in early learning success. Enjoy! ~ Donna Kim-Brand

「ジェイン・フラーガンの "いそがしい わんこの いちにち" は見ているだけで楽しくなるような、可愛さいっぱいの本よ。特に目を引くのはハスキーのエラ！いろんな愛らしいポーズをしたエラが、全ページにカラフルに載ってるの。そんな可愛い子犬のエラとの共通点は何かな？って読んでる子供達に問いかけながらお話が進むの。どんな子でも絶対に、また読んでって何回もおねだりしてくるわよ。」ヒヤグハ・コーヘン（Hiyaguha Cohen）

Jayne Flaagan's book "Doggy's Busy Day" is a charming visual treat, featuring the photogenic husky, Ella. Filled with full-page color photos of Ella in numerous lovable poses, the book asks young readers to notice the similarities between the pup and themselves. This book is sure to be requested over and over by any child. ~ Hiyaguha Cohen

"いそがしい わんこの いちにち" を私の家族に捧げます。写真のためにエラが
"大げさポーズ" を取るよう惜しみない協力をしてくれた家族のみんなに。

"Doggy's Busy Day" is dedicated to my family, who helped encourage
Ella to "ham it up" for the pictures included in this book.

ジェイン・フラーガンは30年以上にわたり幼児教育について学び経験を重ねてきたエキスパート。
喜びと充実感を感じて、この分野での仕事に打ち込んでいます。
フラーガンはノーダコタ出身ですが、満を持して、数年前にミネソタに移住。
3人の子供達は独立して、現在は、夫とおっちょこちょい犬のエラとの3人暮らしを楽しんでいます。

"いそがしい わんこの いちにち" を気に入ってもらえましたら、Amazon にレビューを頂けますと大変嬉しく思います。他の子供達にも、わんこのエラを楽しんでいただけるきっかけになりますように！

エラの他の本も見ていただければ光栄です！わんこのエラと著者ジェインより

ジェイン・フラーガンのウェブサイトはこちらから：www.ellathedoggy.com
連絡はこちらからも受け付けております：djflaagan@gra.midco.net

Jayne Flaagan has over 30 years of experience and education in Early Childhood Education.
She receives much joy and satisfaction working in this genre.
Flaagan grew up in North Dakota and made the big move to Minnesota many years ago.
She lives with her husband and a goofy dog named Ella. She has three grown children.

If you enjoyed *"Doggy's Busy Day,"* I would very much appreciate your leaving a review with Amazon.
This will help other families learn about Ella the doggy too!

Also, don't forget to look for Ella's other books!
Thank you!   Ella (the doggy) and Jayne (the author)

Jayne Flaagan's web site is: www.ellathedoggy.com.   You can contact her at djflaagan@gra.midco.net

読者の皆様、本書を手に取っていただきまして、ありがとうございます。
ささやかではありますが、プレゼントを準備致しました。楽しんでいただけると幸いです。

1. "いそがしい わんこの いちにち" 無料オーディオブックへのリンク
(http://ellathedoggy.com/wp-content/uploads/2016/01/DoggyFindsHerBone-audio-track.mp3)

2. クリエイティブに楽しむエラの塗り絵
(http://ellathedoggy.com/wp-content/uploads/2015/04/coloring-pagespdfapirl17pdf.pdf)

Because we appreciate you as a reader, please accept our gifts to you, which include…

1. A link to receive a FREE audio book of "Doggy's Busy Day"
(http://ellathedoggy.com/wp-content/uploads/2016/01/DoggyFindsHerBone-audio-track.mp3)

2. FREE coloring pages of Ella to print and color
(http://ellathedoggy.com/wp-content/uploads/2015/04/coloring-pagespdfapirl17pdf.pdf)

2014年出版。文章、カバーデザイン、挿し絵の著作権は Jayne Flaagan に帰属します。)
© 2014 Jayne Flaagan Cover Design © 2014 Jayne Flaagan, photography by Jayne Flaagan

著者からの書面による許可なく、本書の全部または一部の無断複写、あらゆる検索システムでの保存、コピー・スキャン・その他手段でのデジタル化等による譲渡並びに配信など、著者の権利を侵害する行為は一切禁止されています。Copyright © 2014 Jayne Flaagan Cover Design © 2014 Jayne Flaagan Pictures by Jayne Flaagan（or, 2014年出版。文章、カバーデザイン、写真の著作権は Jayne Flaaganに帰属します。)

No part of this publication may be reproduced in whole or in part, or stored in a retrieval system, or transmitted in any form or by any means, electronic, mechanical, photocopying, recording or otherwise, without written permission of the author.

Copyright © 2014 Jayne Flaagan Cover Design   © 2014 Jayne Flaagan , photography by Jayne Flaagan

この子は　エラ。

おめめが　ふたつ。おみみが　ふたつ。

おはなは　ひとつで、おくちも　ひとつ。

きみと　おんなじ。

This is Ella the Doggy.

She has two eyes. She has two ears.

She has one nose. She has one mouth.

Just like you

エラのあしは　4ほんで、　しっぽが　いっぽん。

きみのあしは　なんぼん？

しっぽは　あるの？

Ella has four legs and one tail.

How many legs do you have?

Do you have a tail?

あさ おきると、
エラは おおーきく のびをするの。

きみは のびをするとき、 どんなきもち？

When Ella wakes up in the morning, she gives herself a very big stretch!

How does that feel when you stretch?

めが さめると、 おなかが とってもぺっこぺこ。 あさごはん まだかな。

すっごく おなかがへったよ。 くちびるを ペロッ。

きみは ごはんを たべるとき、 よだれかけを するのかな？

Ella is very hungry when she wakes up, so she gets ready for breakfast.

She is so hungry, she is licking her lips.

Do you wear a bib when you eat?

ときどき エラは おすわりして、
ごはんを おねだり。

「ちょうだい」は いえないの。
だって いぬは おしゃべり でき
ないからね。

きみは なにか ほしいとき、 な
んて いうの？

Sometimes Ella will sit up and ask for food.

She cannot say "please" because doggies cannot talk.

What do you say when you want something?

エラは　しろいボウルで　あさごはんを　たべるの。
ボウルは　はがたで　いっぱい。
エラのは　は　するどいし、
ボウルで　あそぶのが　だいすき　だから。

Ella eats her breakfast from a white bowl.

The bowl is all chewed up because she has sharp teeth and she likes to play with it.

いぬは　おみずを　いっぱい　のむの。

エラは　あおいボウルで　おみずを　のむよ。

きみは　おみずを　のむのに　なにを　つかう？

Doggies drink lots of water too.

Ella drinks from a blue bowl.

What do you use to drink water?

あ、エラが　おさんぽに　いくよ。
おお　はしゃぎ！

Ella is going on a walk now.
She is very excited!

さわやかな くうき、 おそとを あるくの だいすき。

おおきく げんきに なるために、
きみは どんな うんどうを するのかな？

She loves to walk outside in the fresh air.

What do you do to exercise
so you can grow big and strong?

そとが　さむくても、　エラは　おさんぽ。

きみが　すんでいるところでは　ゆきは　ふるのかな？

Even when it is cold outside, Ella takes a walk.

Do you have snow where you live?

おさんぽのあと、

きみは　どこで　きゅうけいするの？

After her walk Ella is tired, so she naps in the sun.

Where do you rest?

エラは　いま　ちょっと　かなしいの。

だれか　あそんで　くれないかな。

Ella is sad right now.

She wants someone to play with.

エラは　しあわせ。おともだちを　みつけたから！
かなしいとき、きみは　どんな　かおを　するの？
うれしいときは、　どんな　かおかな？

Now Ella is happy because she sees a friend!

What does your face look like when you are sad?

How does your face look when you are happy?

これは　ちいさかったときの　エラ。
おともだちの　デイジーと　あそんでいるところ。
きみの　おともだちの　なまえは　なに？

This is Ella when she was smaller.

She is playing with her friend Daisy.

What are the names of your friends?

ときどき　エラは　おともだちのみんなと　ピクニックに　いくよ。
きみは　ピクニックに　いったら　なにを　たべるの？

Sometimes Ella has picnics with her people friends.
What do you eat when you go on a picnic?

？あ！　おかしなこと　してるのは　だれ？

きみが　おかしなことをするのは　どんなとき

Look who is being silly!

What do you do when you act silly?

エラは　ゲームで　あそぶのが　すき。

ときどき　エラは　つなひきを　するよ。

Ella likes to play games too.

Sometimes she plays a game called *Tug-Of-War*.

これは　エラが　べつのゲームで　あそんでいるところ。
ごほうびを　にぎってる　てを　さがさなきゃいけないの。
エラが　ごほうびを　さがすの、　てつだってくれる？

Here is Ella playing another game.
She has to find the hand that holds her treat.
Can you help her find the treat?

エラは　ダンスも　じょうず。

きみは　どんなダンスを　するの？

Ella is a good dancer.

How do you dance?

たまには ほねを かじって ただ おやすみするだけ。 それも いいよね。

Sometimes Ella just likes to rest and chew on her bone...

それから　たまには　ボールで　あそぶの。

and sometimes she plays with a ball.

エラは　みんなに　キスするのも　すき。

Ella likes to give kisses to people...

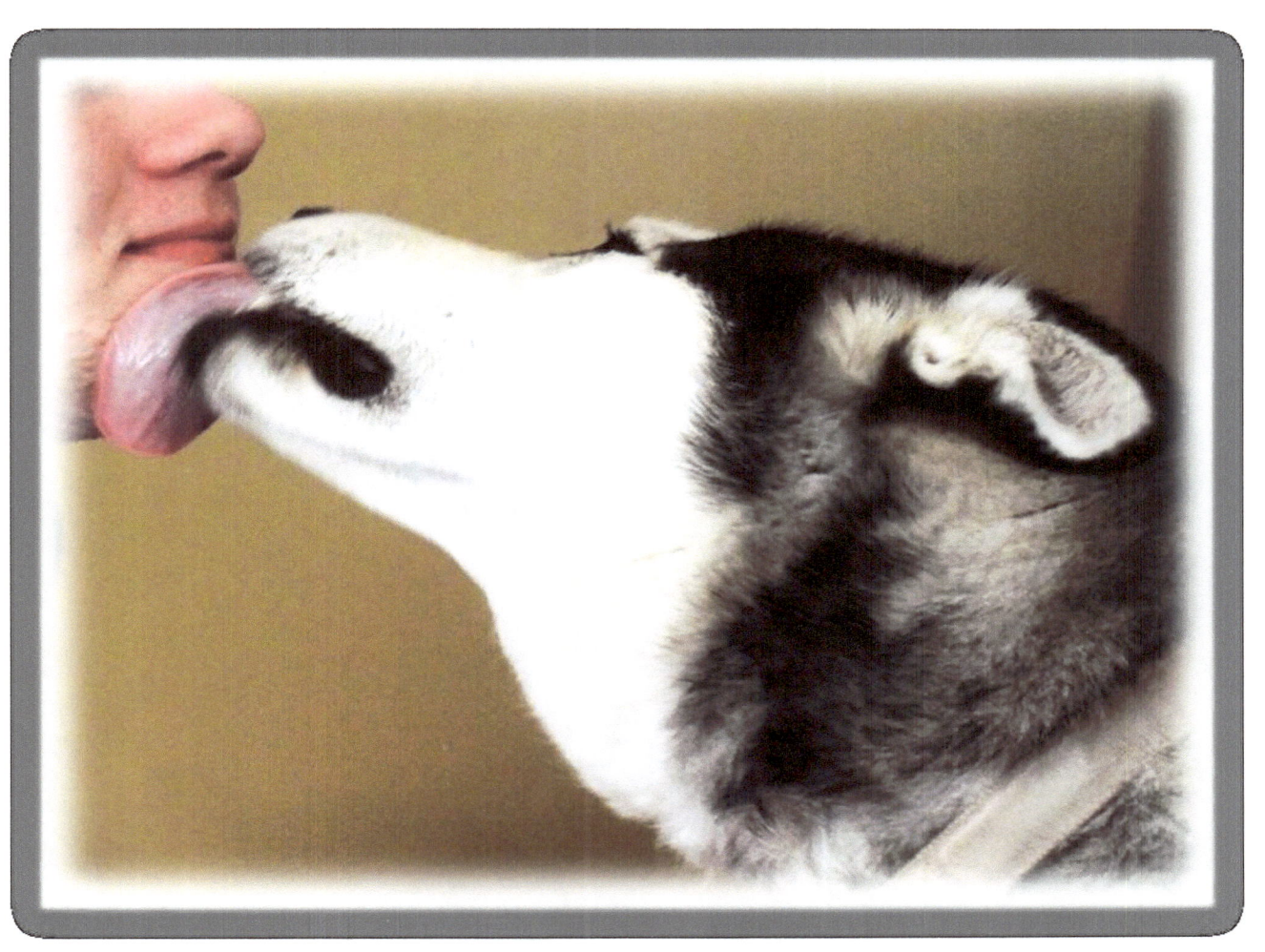

ながーいベロで！

with her long tongue!

エラは　みんなに　ハグするのも　すき。

Ella likes to hug people too.

きょう、　エラは　くるまに　のるよ。

あ！　エラ、　シートベルトを　しめてない！

Today Ella is going for a ride in the car.

Oh no! She is not wearing a seat belt!

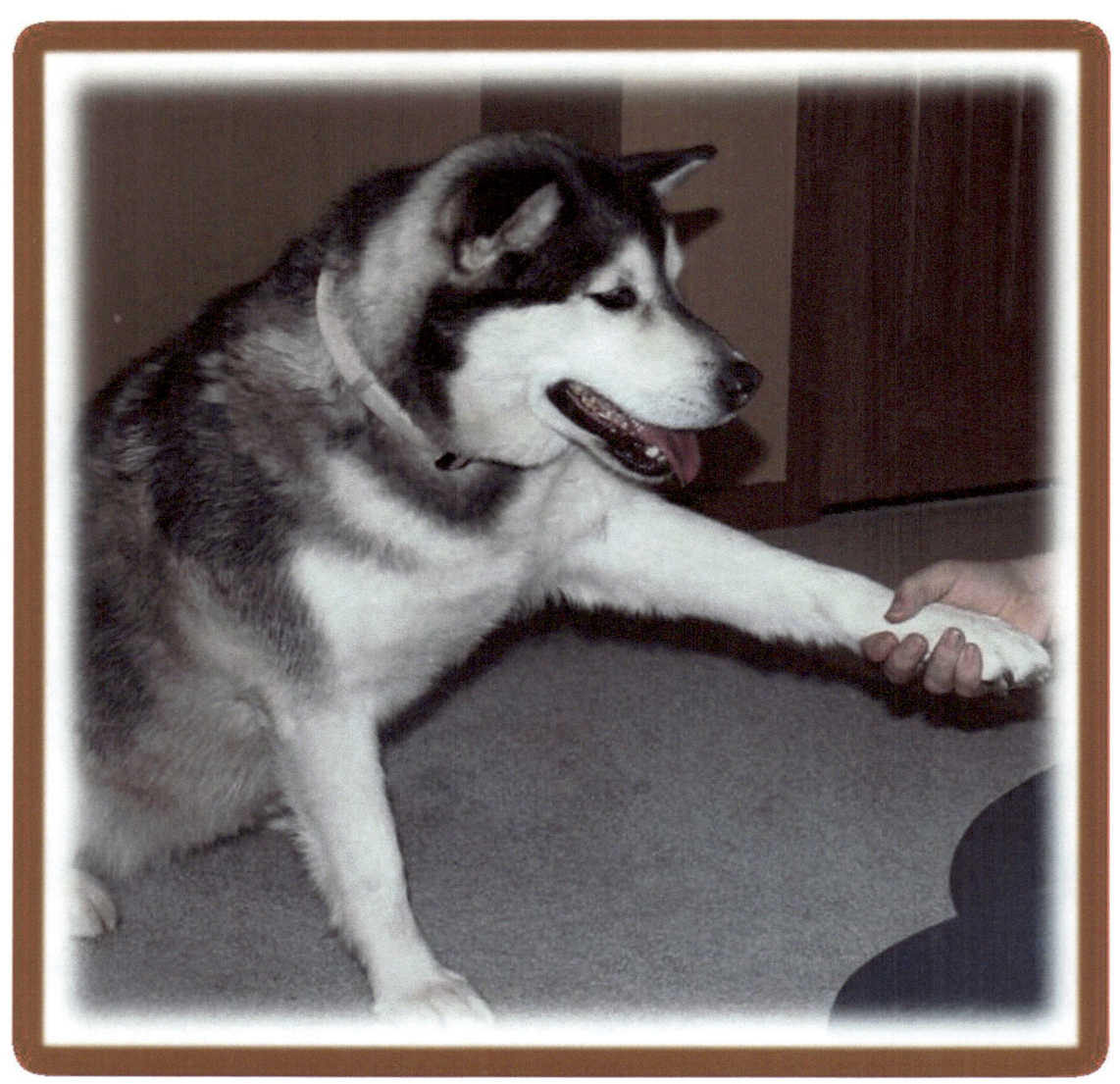

はじめてのひとたちと　あうときは、　まえあしで　あくしゅ。

When she meets new people, Ella shakes with her paw…

…それから、とってもうれしいときは　ハイファイブするの。

…and she gives a "*high five*" when she is excited.

きみは　まえあしで　あくしゅするの？　それとも　おてて？
どうやって「ハイファイブ」するか　しってる？

Do you shake with a paw or with a hand?

Do you know how to give "*high fives*"?

エラ、　きょうは　とってもいそがしいひ　だったね。

It has been a very busy day for Ella.

あれ？　エラは　どこにいったの？

But wait...where is she going?

いた！　まどの　そとを　みてるみたい。

あしたも　いそがしいひに　なるかな　って　いろんなこと　かんがえてるの。

Here is Ella!　She is looking out the window.

Ella is thinking about all of the things that will keep her busy tomorrow!

わんこの　エラ

Ella the Doggy

"いそがしい わんこの いちにち" を気に入ってもらえましたら、Amazon にレビューを頂けますと大変嬉しく思います。

他の子供達にも、わんこのエラを楽しんでいただけるきっかけになりますように！

Thank you!
どうぞよろしくお願い致します。

Ella (the doggy) and Jayne (the author)

わんこのエラと著者ジェインより

www.ellathedoggy.com

Ella's Other Books:

[Doggy's Busy Day](#)

[Doggy Finds Her Bone](#)

[Doggy Loves Autumn](#)

[Doggy's Minnesota Winter](#)

Doggy Celebrates Christmas

[El Día Ocupado de la Perrita/Doggy's Buy Day](#)
(Bilingual book in both Spanish and English)

[Hundis Aufregender Tag/Doggy's Busy Day](#)
(Bilingual book in both German and English)

[La Journée Chargée de la Petite/Doggy's Busy Day](#)
(Bilingual book in both French and English)

[Pracowity Dzień Pieska/Doggy's Busy Day](#)
(Bilingual book in both Polish and English)